Being Transparent

With Yourself, God, and Others

Leader's

Discussion Guide

Susan M. Sims

This discussion guide is dedicated to leaders in our churches desiring to see small groups dig deeper in their relationships with God. May God continue to bless your efforts.

Contents

A PERSONAL NOTE...

Welcome! I'm glad to have you join me on this journey of our small groups becoming more transparent with each other.

Bible studies and small groups are vital to the growth of Christians because they are the accountability groups which keep us focused and headed in the right direction. Small groups, whether Bible studies, Sunday school classes, or men's/women's groups, help shape us and form our thoughts and ideas as we explore God and what He has for us. Likewise, we tend to compare ourselves with those around us. If we base our thoughts of ourselves on those not in an active relationship with Christ, we will fall short on most days. We need the support of godly people in our lives, whether or not we like to admit our need for others.

God has called us into relationships with others, just as He desires a relationship from us; therefore, relationships are not an option and are a must if we are to truly desire God in our lives. If we are going to actively pursue this concept of transparency, we must be willing to open our doors and safe places as the Holy Spirit leads. *Realize that being transparent with others is not a free-for-all in telling every single person our story.* Jesus had 12 disciples in His ministry. Even within these 12 men, He had a select group of three men with whom He shared more than the others. Let's allow Him to be our example in our journey with transparency.

My desire for wanting to write *Being Transparent with Yourself, God, and Others* stemmed from something that happened in my life. Our church had a ministry which included helping people recovering from addictions and those coming out of jail. It was energizing to see their desire and affection for God. They were unashamed of how they felt about God and about what others thought of them when they worshipped because worship for them was personal and between God and them.

Their desire to grow closer to God required them to ask questions that revealed where they had been previously in their past. Even though they were not proud of where they had been, they still realized they needed help or clarification for their next step in walking with God. This openness was very refreshing to me as a leader because I had been in some groups that considered a small group a place to catch up on life happenings and admitting they didn't do their lesson for the week. It was very unfulfilling to me on my journey. I wanted to walk with those who were seriously ready to take their relationship with God to the next level because, when I was with people seriously committed to drawing closer to God, I was more apt to be committed.

Being serious for God is just as contagious as not being serious about God. You choose one way or the other.

Part of the responsibility of the leader is to be real and transparent, again, as the Lord leads, so that others are more willing to go there with you. I pray this leader's discussion guide will further enable you and your group to go a bit deeper in discovering who it is God created you to be, allow you to fall in love with the Creator of this universe, and see how you can better interact with others around you. May God bless you on this journey and draw you closer to Him.

I would love to hear from you and answer any questions you have along the way. Feel free to connect with me on my website: www.susanmsims.com

In Him,

Susan

USING THIS DISCUSSION GUIDE...

Should you be wondering where to begin in leading a small group, this guide is for you! In the book, *Being Transparent with Yourself, God, and Others*, there are questions at the end of each chapter for participants to answer on their own time. Throughout this discussion guide, these questions are incorporated within the weekly lessons and the actual numbers of the questions have been left for you to help you follow along with which question is being asked. Along with these questions, quotes from the book (indicated by the book's page numbers) and other discussion questions have been written for you to aid in the flow of your class time. These ideas are simply some suggestions for you in case you get "stuck" in your sharing time. Allow the Holy Spirit to lead you personally with the group with which you've been entrusted.

This study is broken down into seven (7) weeks. The first week is intended to be an introduction and "social" time to allow for some discussion among your members. Some groups who have been meeting together for many years may be able to forgo this week. Other groups who have new members will need this week to allow members to get to know each other. Based on your group, you might want to take more time with each lesson.

Once you have decided how many weeks your group will need, you will need to advertise up to 4-6 weeks before your class begins. Here are some blurbs you can use:

> *When life happens, where do you turn, with whom do you share, and how much do you handle on your own? How open and transparent does God call us to be on a daily basis?*

> *Come explore the freedom of living a transparent life as God intended and watch your relationship with God grow deeper than before!*

> *Do you struggle with transparency? Discover some barriers we must overcome in our journey to living a transparent life.*

Here are some suggestions I have used successfully in the past with my small groups:

1. *Bring in snacks for the group.* Others in the group could bring food, as well. This can be as simple as chocolate chip cookies or brownies. Food provides a comfort and a distraction for some people. It gives them something to do with their hands if they are nervous or anxious about the topic of transparency. This is very helpful for the first time the group meets and can be fun to do throughout the rest of the study. You can even pass around a sign-up sheet for the following weeks if your group loves the idea of snacks.

2. *Provide paper and pens for people in the group.* Again, this gives them something to do with their hands and provides a distraction.

3. *Provide a sign-in sheet and ask for their names, cell numbers, and emails.* This will give you a class roster so you can communicate with them throughout the week. If all members are active on Facebook and prefer Facebook, you could setup a Facebook group. Otherwise, ask what form of communication your group prefers and a simple weekly email or text would work well. This is a great avenue of communication for prayer requests shared during the week.

4. *Agree upon a start and stop time and stick to it firmly.* The idea of timing provides safe boundaries for those feeling uncomfortable in a group. It also helps the chatty members realize they cannot talk very long. This gives you an out when you need to stop them on their drawn-out story. Again, how you remind them to shorten their story will depend on how well you know them.

5. *Remember to keep your talking short.* Just like you don't want one person in the group to monopolize the conversation, people in the group might just need you to stop talking for a few minutes before they are willing to talk. Those more apt to be quiet will not rush to talk when you only take a breath for five seconds. Be comfortable with silence!

6. *Share prayer requests and praises with the group.* This can be done either at the beginning or at the end. You will know what is best depending on your group. I have found that if a group is

very chatty, you can focus them better if the requests are done at the beginning. There is always an exception to this rule, but it has worked most of the time for me. In order to keep within the boundaries of your end time, it's sometimes easier to cut parts of your lesson out and save it until next week rather than to cut short on the prayer requests.

7. *Remember to pray for those in your group.* Prayer is a vital part of any small group. Pray that God will give you the words to say to those who will attend your study. Also, pray He will give you the wisdom to not speak the words you think are appropriate, but may not be helpful for those attending.

8. *Follow-up on prayer requests.* Ask how the situation is progressing and ask how the person is feeling about how it's progressing. This is accountability in the making! Again, emailing prayer requests during the week puts a reminder in front of your group that they are accountable to others.

Let's get started!

WEEK 1

Introduction and Discovering One Another

The Plan: This lesson is intended to be an introductory time for you and the group.

- Open the meeting time with prayer.

    o   This will move everyone closer to the right frame of mind and give pause to their hectic schedules, allowing a time for them to breathe and relax.

    o   This allows the group to know that even though this night will be socially oriented, there is also a meaning and purpose to this time.

- Introduce yourself to group.

    o   There may be people who are not familiar with you or your desire to lead small groups.

    o   Remember what you share, how much or how little, will determine how much others are willing to share.

- o Share a funny memory you have about your life that others may not know about, especially if you are a very familiar group.

- Give a quick update on the book and what interested you about the book. Introducing transparency as a "subject" will make it feel a bit less emotional and less threatening. Be honest about your views on transparency...do you struggle with it, find it perplexing, or actually like transparency. Let the group know you are all on this journey together.

- Set some rules and have participants sign the "Small Group Covenant" (located in the *Resources* section in the back of the book).

    - o What happens in the group stays in the group.

    - o You do not have permission to share what someone else shares unless they give the group permission.

    - o This is a safe place.

    - o Remind them that sharing what is not theirs to share is gossiping, and gossiping is called a sin in the Bible.

- Transparency requires some vulnerability and some subjects might get uncomfortable. Allow people to get vulnerable. Also, allow others who can't go there the freedom to express their discomfort. This is what an accountability group is about...willing to be uncomfortable with one another. Saying this upfront to your group will give freedom in sharing and freedom in silence.

- After rules and expectations for the group have been set, go around the room and ask each person to share something about themselves with the group. This will give the group a bit more information on who is in the group. Plus, this allows you to observe how people see themselves in their own eyes.

  o Some examples:

    ▪ Their name
    ▪ Married or single
    ▪ Have kids or pets
    ▪ What they do: job, stay-at-home parent, retired

- Realize that some people find their identity in who they are and what they do, so it's fun to ask "imaginative" questions to help them feel free to talk and not to be dependent upon what they see themselves as being (by the questions mentioned above). Examples:

  o For those younger: When you are retired, what do you plan to do?

  o For those retired: What was something you were really glad you did when you were younger?

  o For those older: What advice do you have to those younger in the group?

  o For those younger: What do you need from those older in the group?

- Provide paper and pens to the group. Ask them to write a letter to their younger self. What advice would you give to yourself when you were 15? 21? 30? 40? This will get them thinking about their life experiences. Were they too hard on themselves? Should they have listened to their parents more or found better examples to be their friends? Did someone try to help them and they pushed them aside?

- o Let them know they will not share this information tonight and to hold on to this until the end of class. This writing will give them a safe place to share.

- Ask the class why they wanted to do this study on transparency.

  - o Ask the group what drew them to study this topic.

  - o Do they think this will be easy or hard for them?

  - o Are they already aware if they struggle with transparency? If so, is it with themselves, God, others, or a combination?

  - o Was there a certain time in their lives when they struggled more than others?

  - o Remind them that you are all on this journey together and remind them, again, that what is said in the room stays in the room.

- Instruct the class to read chapter one and to write their life story (at the end of chapter one). They may be able to use some of what they wrote on their "advice to their younger self" in this life story writing.

- o If you need to fill more of the meeting time, allow them to write some of their story in class.

- o Alternate idea: Have the class take a personality test. A person's personality plays a large part in how they interact with themselves, God, and others. You could take the test as a group and discuss it together or have the class members take it on their own during the week. http://www.sagestrategies.biz/documents/FiveMinutePersonalityTestforclass.pdf is a great resource for this test. Other suggestions are located in the RESOURCES section in the back of the book.

- End with prayer and/or prayer requests (if you prefer to save them until now). Pray and thank God for bringing this group together and praise Him for what He has in store for this group.

- End on time! ☺

WEEK 2

Chapter 1. *What is Transparency?*

The Plan. This lesson is intended to last one week.

Welcome everyone to the group. Ask for prayer requests (or this can be done at the end of the class time). Lead in prayer and ask God to bless the discussion you're about to have. Being transparent and open with a group dynamic requires the guidance and direction of the Holy Spirit. Pray specifically for this in your group. Pray for the discussion to be guided by Him. This will give some direction to the attendees that this is a sacred and special group and what is shared is not intended to go outside the room, unless permission is given.

Do a small introduction of anyone new to your group. You could even allow those who attended last week to do a short intro, as well, so the new people will not feel put on-the-spot.

Remind the group that what is shared in the group stays in the group. This is a safe place for people to practice sharing, as well as a safe place to hold others accountable.

We often think of transparency as exposing ourselves to others and we are embarrassed. Oftentimes, though, it is simply owning up to what we have done or who we are. When we treat transparency as something we choose to do or be, instead of something being forced upon us, we can see transparency in its fruitful and positive light.

State the definition of transparency:

1. Permitting the uninterrupted passage of light; clear

2. Easy to see through, understand, or recognize; obvious

Many times, we don't think of transparency as obvious. We are to live our lives in such a way that when people see us they will "obviously" know what we will do and/or be.

Ask: Did you struggle with writing your life story or was it easy? This is not a question about their writing skills! Ask if anyone is brave enough to share with the group or to share highlights.

Just like Shakespeare's *Hamlet,* we have to ask the question "to be or not to be" in our lives. We have a choice: will we be transparent or not.

- Remind your class that transparency is an empowering part of their lives. They have the power to share or the power to withhold. This power can be used for the good or the bad; this is their choice.

- Quote from Eleanor Roosevelt: "No one can make you feel inferior without your consent."

- Hamlet ultimately chose death.

Pages 8-9: "When we dismiss the things of life as trivial or not as important compared to what others are facing, we can begin to slowly die inside. This is when the struggle begins. We will have to choose to share a part of our lives we might consider trivial with someone else. The transparency will not only benefit our souls, but it will also benefit those around us who are secretly struggling."

Ask: How have you been helped in the past by other people sharing their struggles? This was them being transparent. We need to return the favor to others by sharing our struggles.

Page 12: "If we are unwilling to share our thoughts with others, we are not only putting ourselves over God in these areas to figure them out on our own, but we are creating masks to those around us. These masks can become stumbling blocks for our friends, children, or most anyone. These little areas we hide from those around us, in fact, are breeding grounds for Satan to work against our desire for a deeper relationship with God."

- When we pretend to have it all together, we are creating an idol for us/them of a perfect life: something unattainable.

- Take a moment and think about some areas in your life that are breeding grounds for Satan. What are your weaknesses or things you might be too ashamed to admit you struggle with?

Ask: What are some ways you try to handle life on your own? Do you tend to handle the smaller or bigger things in life on your own?

Ever feel as though you are "dying" inside? Not sure where to go or with whom to share? Let's look at two examples from the book: Jim and Mary.

Jim: Grew up in church, attended regularly, knew about God, attended Bible studies, good marriage and family, didn't feel connected, felt discontentment, shutting down, trying to handle life on his own.

Mary: Didn't grow up in church, came to church out of desperation, single mom with troubled kids, self-conscious, felt connected in her Bible study group, starting to feel alive again, trying to handle life on her own.

Page 11: "If people are not careful, they can assume they are mature Christians since they have been a Christian for a long time."

Ask: How do you see this last statement panning out in the life of Christians around you?

Page 14: "You see, the longer we go about our lives pretending, or not acknowledging the problems, our knots are simply getting tighter and the struggle to free ourselves becomes more difficult."

- Whether in your life, or in the life of those you know, how do you see this working in regards to telling lies and keeping all the stories straight?

- Problems are much easier to overcome if we face them head-on as soon as we find out what the problem is.

  o We are called to deal with any sin in our life as soon as we know it is sin.

Ask: How might Jim and Mary have reacted to the following quote from Tennessee Williams: "We have to distrust each other. It is our only defense against betrayal"?

In fear of transparency, we can tend to revert to isolation. This is not how God intended us to live our lives. He made us for relationship. This relationship can provide the accountability we need, but this requires trust.

Finish the lesson by reading the last couple of paragraphs in chapter one about being accountable and sharing our lives with others. You can't share something you don't know anything about; therefore, you need to know who God created you to be and who you have allowed yourself to become. Who you are right now might not be the person God intended you to be. In the next couple of chapters, we will look at how the expectations we have of ourselves both mentally and physically can impact who we've become; whether for good or bad.

End with the Group Transparency Exercise at the end of chapter one.

> *Group Transparency Exercise:*
> Whether your life's story is more like Jim or Mary's, in your next group prayer time, have every group participant give a personal prayer request. The context of each request should reveal a personal weakness or need, as well as, how God might answer their prayer to help them.

Encourage the class to read chapter two for next week and to answer the questions at the end of the chapter.

End with prayer and/or prayer requests (if you prefer to save them until now).

End on time! ☺

WEEK 3

Chapter 2: Mental Transparency and Expectations

The Plan: This lesson is intended to last one week.

Welcome everyone to the group. Ask for prayer requests (or this can be done at the end of the class time). Lead in prayer and ask God to bless the discussion you're about to have. Being transparent and open with a group dynamic requires the guidance and direction of the Holy Spirit. Pray specifically for this in your group. Pray for the discussion to be guided by Him. This will give some direction to the attendees that this is a sacred and special group and what is shared is not intended to go outside the room, unless permission is given.

> **Ask:** What is your definition of mental transparency and expectations?

Read the quote from Dan Miller: "When we are not true to ourselves, to our unique God-given characteristics, we lose the power of authenticity, creativity, imagination, and innovation. Our life becomes performance-based, setting the stage for compromise in all other areas of our lives."

Ask: What does being true to ourselves have to do with mental transparency? (Possible answer: We see our lives a certain way and sometime we forget who we are as a person if we don't reflect on our life and how we're living.)

Ask: How do transparency and the mind work together? What are some examples of difficulty in being transparent when you are confused about where you are in life?

Ask: What are some ways your life is, or has been, performance-based?

Page 21: "In absence of clearly defined goals, we become strangely loyal to performing daily acts of trivia." –Author Unknown

Ask the group about goals. Do you set yearly goals? Why or why not? The purpose of this question is to get the group to talk. You are allowing conversation to happen in a safe environment. The group members can divulge as much information as they desire.

- Should the group not have any desire to talk about themselves, ask them if they know of another person who sets goals and if they are effective in keeping their goals or not.

Talk about the "high blood sugars" of life and its waste products in the life of Jim and Mary. What waste products do you see in your life: irritability, impatience, numbness? What are some things in your life that bring "stable" or "lower" blood sugars? (e.g., prayer, church, talking with your best friend, family)

Proverbs 3:5 – "Trust in the LORD with all your heart and do not lean on your own understanding."

Ask. What is the value of trusting God instead of our own understanding?

Page 25: "To be able to share ourselves with others requires some introspection…this questioning of ourselves takes a lot of courage."

Page 27: "Whether Jim or Mary's lives had turned out as they originally planned, one thing they had in common was certain expectations of their lives. Likewise, we all have some expectations of our lives."

1. Name three expectations you have for your life?

2. Are your expectations being met currently, or do you feel unfulfilled?

3. What expectations of your life did not happen? How does it make you feel to write them down? Relieved? Bitter? Angry?

Page 25: "Like Jim, we may feel we have failed if we are not content with our lives." Is this true for you?

4. Do you resent your life or are you content?

Page 26: How do you relate to the example of the puzzle? When do you choose the first option and when do you choose the second one?

Page 27: "Contentment is more about asking the question, 'Do I trust God enough with my life so that whatever circumstances I am in I can fully rely upon Him for my heart's desires?' Ultimately, am I satisfied where I am?"

Ask. How do you deal with introspection? Do you take time for introspection?

5.   What areas of your life bring you joy?

Page 29: Regarding the story of the child carrying garbage bags, what are some circumstances in your life where God has asked you to do something and, in your hurry and frustration, you try to rush to get it done and make yourself miserable in the process?

Page 31: Read through the D.L. Moody quote: "There are many of us that are willing to do great things for the Lord, but few of us are willing to do little things."

Ask: What are the little things in your life? Do you struggle with doing the little things?

Page 32: "We try to filter parts of our lives so others will see us in a certain light. Could it be that we have worn a mask so long so others cannot see us, that we have even fooled ourselves? No wonder we become surprised at what we say and how we act."

Ask: Do you know anyone that fooled themselves into thinking they were someone else?

Pages 33–35: Review the plant story and ask the following:

- What areas in your life did taking shortcuts have a negative impact upon your life?

- What kind of shortcuts are you currently trying to take in life?

6.   What areas of your life choke and restrict you?

   o   What roots in your life are choking the seeds God has planted in your life?

7.   Do you feel God has expectations for your life? If so, how do you feel about God's expectations?

8.   Is it easy for you to trust God with your life? What makes it hard or easy for you to trust Him?

Page 38: "I realized all my ideas, hopes, and dreams were nothing apart from God. Apart from God they were all about me. I was tired of me and wanted Him. This began a great year of learning to lean on God and God alone. Being made in God's greater image became my expectation."

When God is our expectation, it can be easier to trust Him because we expect Him to be God. God = trust.

Page 38: "...God showed me my expectations of doing things on my own were so below what He intended for me."

Ask: Do you realize that your expectations are generally below what God intends and desires for you? How can we get past this and learn to expect what He intends?

Page 40: Matthew 11:28 states "Come to Me, all who are weary and heavy-laden, and I will give you rest." God desires for us to come to Him at all times. Go over the two definitions of weary in that paragraph and then pose the question, "What in our lives make us tired?"

Group Transparency Exercise:
Choose one person and give a few moments for everyone to share what they feel God's expectations of that person might be. Do this same exercise with the remaining group members. It might be beneficial to have someone record the expectations of the group.

Mental transparency requires a deeper introspection than many of us have time to do on a yearly basis. We will not be able to share with others who we are if we don't even know "us" ourselves. Discuss among the group ways to incorporate introspection of our "expectations of life" to better understand ourselves and who God desires us to become. Ultimately, we do this pondering because we want to be effective for God's Kingdom. We must throw off all hindrances and come to God with our baggage and embrace His expectations of us.

Page 41: Read paragraph: "You see, God does not ask me to 'do' for Him…"

Page 42: Close by reading the last paragraph.

Encourage the class to read chapter three for next week and to answer the questions at the end of the chapter.

End with prayer and/or prayer requests (if you prefer to save them until now).

End on time! ☺

WEEK 4

Chapter 3: Physical Health and Transparency

The Plan: This lesson is intended to last one week.

Welcome everyone to the group. Ask for prayer requests (or this can be done at the end of the class time). Lead in prayer and ask God to bless the discussion you're about to have. Being transparent and open with a group dynamic requires the guidance and direction of the Holy Spirit. Pray specifically for this in your group. Pray for the discussion to be guided by Him. This will give some direction to the attendees that this is a sacred and special group and what is shared is not intended to go outside the room, unless permission is given.

Our physical health affects how much we can accomplish in one day, how well we can focus on the tasks at hand, and what our mood can be depending on how we feel. Most people do not think of physical health affecting transparency, but it does.

Pages 46–48: Story of Megan. Have you gone through times in your life when you just felt "off" whether emotionally or spiritually, and then realized you were "off" simply because you were sick or worn-out?

Pages 48–50: Story of Ron. Our hotels are our bodies.

1. How does your hotel need cleaning today? What needs to be thrown away from your life and what needs to be organized?

Page 51: "Upon review of Megan and Ron's story, Megan struggled to not lose control over her situation while Ron struggled through his situation and achieved a completed hotel."

   Ask: When you go through a hard time, how do you react? Fight or flight?

We all react to situations differently. Sometimes the same person will react differently to different situations. It is important to know how we react and why. Knowing this will empower us in future situations. It's time to ask some personal questions that might seem a bit out of place at first, but hang on until the end. You'll be happy you did.

Page 52: "The idea our body is used to serve God and to complete His purposes for our lives requires us to be transparent with ourselves and our bodies."

2. When you look in a mirror, how do you feel about your body and about how you look?

Page 52: "When we struggle in any part of our lives, this affects how we interact with others and our ability to be transparent with them."

   Ask: Can you apply this quote from page 52 to your answer on question #2 above?

Page 54: "Transparency requires us to know why we do things and what our motives might be."

3. Who shaped your view on beauty and "looking good"? Does your view need a new perspective? How?

4. What do you do to take care of yourself physically? Are you able to fulfill what God desires for you to do in life? What areas of your life cause you to struggle with taking care of your body?

Page 54: Lewis Thomas quote: "As a people, we have become obsessed with Health. There is something fundamentally, radically unhealthy about all of this. We do not seem to be seeking more exuberance in living as much as staving off failure, putting off dying. We have lost all confidence in the human body."

5. Do you struggle with "health" as an idol? If so, in what ways?

6. What daily habits are good and bad to your body, health, and relationships?

Page 55: We need to keep things in perspective and ask ourselves this question, "Do we take care of our bodies well enough to fulfill God's purpose for our lives?"

Page 59: "Anything that negatively affects our ability to serve God with all our heart, soul, mind, and strength is a detriment to our spiritual transparent journey. We must continually ask ourselves what is drawing us away from God and all He desires for us."

Paul wrote a letter to the Corinthians about how their culture was distracting them spiritually as they were giving their bodies up through prostitution to the goddess Aphrodite. He claimed we could not be one with evil and one with God at the same time. Jesus also warns that we cannot serve two masters. Paul points out that our distraction can lead to idol worship and lead us away from God.

7. If Paul wrote a personal letter to you, what would be your distraction or Aphrodite? What steps can you take today to ease that distraction?

Page 60: What happens when our distractions are the mere circumstances we've been dealt with in life?" (e.g., sickness, caring for aging parents, caring for small kids, work, church)

Page 62: "When it comes to God healing us from ourselves and from our desires, we tend to push back. It's almost as though we avoid Doctor God. We busy ourselves with busyness and distractions so we do not have to face the fact that we are sick.

Romans 7:14-20: For we know that the Law is spiritual, but I am of flesh, sold into bondage to sin. For what I am doing, I do not understand; for I am not practicing what I would like to do, but I am doing the very thing I hate. But if I do the very thing I do not want to do, I agree with the Law, confessing that the Law is good. So now, no longer am I the one doing it, but sin which dwells in me. For I know that nothing good dwells in me, that is, in my flesh; for the willing is present in me, but the doing of the good is not. For the good that I want, I do not do, but I practice the very evil that I do not want. But if I am doing the very thing I do not want, I am no longer the one doing it, but sin which dwells in me."

8. What do you do in your life that you do not want to do? What are your addictions?

Page 64: "As we become transparent with our life, the question must be asked if we truly desire for God to heal us of our physical condition, our attitudes, or addictions."

Page 65: Read the last paragraph that closes out the chapter.

> *Group Transparency Exercise:*
> In your group, you will have those like Megan, feeling defeated by circumstances, and those like Ron, working through the circumstances. Have each participant name a distraction they face in their personal lives. Have them give an example of how it distracted them within the past week.

Encourage the class to read chapter four for next week and to answer the questions at the end of the chapter.

End with prayer and/or prayer requests (if you prefer to save them until now).

End on time! ☺

WEEK 5

Chapter 4: Transparency with God

The Plan: This lesson is intended to last one week.

Welcome everyone to the group. Ask for prayer requests (or this can be done at the end of the class time). Lead in prayer and ask God to bless the discussion you're about to have. Being transparent and open with a group dynamic requires the guidance and direction of the Holy Spirit. Pray specifically for this in your group. Pray for the discussion to be guided by Him. This will give some direction to the attendees that this is a sacred and special group and what is shared is not intended to go outside the room, unless permission is given.

Page 68: Open by reading Psalm 62:5-8: "My soul, wait in silence for God only, for my hope is from Him. He only is my rock and my salvation, my stronghold; I shall not be shaken. On God my salvation and my glory rest; the rock of my strength, my refuge is in God. Trust in Him at all times. O people; pour out your heart before Him; God is a refuge for us."

Ask: Who is the focus of the verses we just read? Let's read it again. What part of the verses meant the most to you?

1. How do you explain worrying and trusting in God? How do they compare and how are they different?

2. What things do you worry about most on a daily basis?

Page 69: Read Psalm 119:18–20, 24: "Open my eyes, that I may behold wonderful things from Your law. I am a stranger in the earth; do not hide Your commandments from me. My soul is crushed with longing after Your ordinances at all times. Your testimonies also are my delight; they are my counselors."

3. Do you compare your relationship with God to others' relationship with God? How does that hinder or help you?

Have your group members think of the person they looked up to when they were a spiritual infant.

Ask: What positive aspects did they learn from this person? Any negatives?

At times it can be hard to move forward in our relationship with God if we don't know our struggles.

4. What inhibits you from a daily walk with God? Schedules, life choices, or a lack of desire?

Page 70: "As we deepen our relationship with God through our communication, one question we deal with, though, is 'Do we truly trust in God?' Matthew 6:25 and 30 reads, 'For this reason I say to you, do not be worried about your life, as to what you will eat or what you will drink; nor for your body, as to what you will put on. Is not life more than food, and the body more than clothing? But if God so clothes the grass of the field, which is alive today and tomorrow is thrown into the furnace, will He not much more clothe you? You of little faith!'"

Page 71: Did you have a hard time with your scale of 1–10 regarding trusting God?

> **Ask:** Have issues with trust helped or hindered your relationship with God?

5. What are some steps you can do today to help you in your walk with God? (e.g., having quiet time with God, reading the Bible, listening to Christian music, slowing down schedules and commitments)

6. Do you find it easy to pray? Why or why not? What makes praying hard for you?

Ask: How did you learn to pray? Who taught you to pray?

7. Is it easier to pray for yourself or others? Why is this?

Page 77: "The reason why we obtain no more in prayer is because we expect no more. God usually answers us according to our own hearts." –Richard Alleine

- Take a moment to stop and pray. Ask the group to quietly search their hearts and to ask God to widen their expectations of Him. Feel free to have silent prayer first and then you can close the quiet time with a group-led prayer.

8. How do we react to God when difficult circumstances come our way? (e.g., hide, run towards Him through prayer, distract ourselves)

Page 75: "All God wanted was me. He wanted me to fully rest in Him in whatever circumstance."

Ask: How do you feel knowing God wants you? How do you rest in Him?

9. How do you explain our loving God to those in this world when bad things happen?

- Bad times will come. Our faith can be shaken if we do not trust in God. Sometimes it is hard to explain bad things when we are confused ourselves. Ultimately, we must always focus upon God and not our current circumstances. God is good and can only be Who He is: God.

Page 80: Psalm 119:26-27; 33-38 can be our prayer to God during these hard times. These first two verses might be some to memorize.

"I have told of my ways, and You have answered me; teach me Your statues. Make me understand the way of Your precepts, so I will meditate on Your wonders…Teach me, O LORD, the way of Your statutes, and I shall observe it to the end. Give me understanding, that I may observe Your law and keep it with all my heart. Make me walk in the path of Your commandments, for I delight in it. Incline my heart to Your testimonies and not to dishonest gain. Turn away my eyes from looking at vanity, and revive me in Your ways. Establish Your word to Your servant, as that which produces reverence for You."

10. Where are you in your transparency with God?

Page 77: "We must all learn to live in the freedom that God has a special bond with each unique person unlike any other."

Page 85: "I truly believe God would rather have us approaching His throne with questioning than to turn our back on Him."

True transparency gives us the freedom to question God, not out of rebellion, but out of a desire for His understanding.

> *Group Transparency Exercise:*
> Have each member of your group name a specific time in their lives when they struggled to see God as good. Who and/or what allowed or prevented them from overcoming this perception of God not being good?

Encourage the class to read chapter five for next week and to answer the questions at the end of the chapter.

Read Psalm 119:26–27 as you close.

End with prayer and/or prayer requests (if you prefer to save them until now).

End on time! ☺

WEEK 6

Chapter 5: Transparency with Others

The Plan: This lesson is intended to last one week.

Welcome everyone to the group. Ask for prayer requests (or this can be done at the end of the class time). Lead in prayer and ask God to bless the discussion you're about to have. Being transparent and open with a group dynamic requires the guidance and direction of the Holy Spirit. Pray specifically for this in your group. Pray for the discussion to be guided by Him. This will give some direction to the attendees that this is a sacred and special group and what is shared is not intended to go outside the room, unless permission is given.

1. Is your first feeling about being transparent with others positive or negative? Why?

Page 89: It's important to note that "we must turn to God to know how much to open up with others and to whom we share our lives".

Transparency with others can be scary and intimidating. It will be important to reiterate that we are not called to tell everyone our complete story. Jesus had three disciples with whom He was closest to among His twelve disciples. It is okay to have a close group with whom both good times and hard times are shared and lived together. The Holy Spirit will empower us to know when and how much to share with others; however, we must be listening to Him.

Pages 90–91: Second Corinthians 1:3–5, "Blessed be the God and Father of our Lord Jesus Christ, the Father of mercies and God of all comfort, who comforts us in all our affliction so that we will be able to comfort those who are in any affliction with the comfort with which we ourselves are comforted by God. For just as the sufferings of Christ are ours in abundance, so also our comfort is abundant through Christ."

2. How have your interactions of being transparent affected you in your transparency journey?

3. What is the hardest part for you in admitting to others that you are struggling? (e.g., bad experiences that caused you to no longer want to open up, trust issues, pride)

4. How does selfishness inhibit transparency for you?

   • What do you tend to be selfish about...your time, your family secrets, your insecurities?

Pages 93–94: Read Steven Kalas' article.

5. Who has murdered your reputation and how? Did you surrender, give up, decide they can't define your life, or are you still fighting back?

Page 94: "We are not alone in our sufferings and parts of our lives will be lost if we continue to live in this hurt." Our hurt can blind us in our daily living. We must never allow our hurt to blind us and/or become our "idol". Life cannot be built around our hurts. Our hurts can shape us, but we must continually strive to grow in God's grace and mercy.

Ask. Have you ever thought about what you might miss in your life if you continue to live in your hurt?

Page 95. "We will be enslaved to others if we run away from who we are, so we leave it alone and let the accusations die."

Ask. How does caring what others think of us enslave us to them?

- Remember, we must always live for God and not for others.

Page 95. "Often we are so burdened and overwhelmed with other thoughts, images, and concerns that it may take a long time before God's Word has swept all else aside and come through" (Bonhoeffer 1954, 82).

Ask. Do times in your life seem better when you are in God's Word versus times you are not spending time reading the Bible? Do you have examples of the impact God's Word has had in your life?

Matthew 7.4-5. "Or how can you say to your brother, 'Let me take the speck out of your eye,' and behold, the log is in your own eye? You hypocrite, first take the log out of your own eye, and then you will see clearly to take the speck out of your brother's eye."

Page 96. "If we pretend to have it all together, we basically are pretending and living a lie. Doesn't sound much like a Christian, does it?"

6. Do you struggle with perfection? If so, how has this affected your transparency with others?

7. How do you trust others when they have broken your trust?

- If your best friend's heart had been broken, whether through being single, getting a divorce, losing a child or spouse, etc., what advice would you give her regarding trusting someone else in her life? Do you apply this same advice to your life?

Ask: Does your trust of others correlate with your trust of God and/or yourself?

8. Does pride and self-reliance go hand-in-hand for you or are they two different issues?

Page 99: "The desire for more things and the best things is simply a mask we use to fill this hole, and can become a downfall for people as it replaces the relationships God intended for our lives."

9. What impact has materialism had on your life? Do you say it impacts your transparency with others in a positive or negative way?

Page 100: "Stuff literally clutters our view of others and we struggle to see the heart of people like God sees them."

Ask: Do you see this to be true as you look at others and possibly compare your life with them?

Page 100: Discuss the quote by David Hume, "Beauty in things exists in the mind which contemplates them."

Page 102: "As Christians, it is vital for us to be honest with ourselves on the impact others have on our lives, whether positively or negatively."

Discuss how others have impacted your life. Maybe this week you could send a card or email and thank them for what they mean to you.

Page 103: "Asking for prayer over a circumstance is not a sign of weakness; rather, it is a sign of great faith. You are admitting to leaving your problems in God's hands and addressing the fact that it is hard to leave it there. This is the very reason you ask for prayer."

> **Ask:** Does this change how and/or why you share prayer requests in the future? Does this change your outlook on others as they share requests?

> 10. How has your prayer life impacted your ability to be transparent with others?

Page 105: "I don't think it's possible to be truly transparent and open with others if we don't have our relationship with God on the right track. If we do not understand who we are, then how can we interact with others? ... we must constantly remain in God."

> **Ask:** Do you recognize the vitality of God being in our sharing with others for it to be authentically real? Is this concept of God being with us freeing to you or scary? Sometimes, knowing He's in control is freeing, frightful, and/or overwhelming.

Jesus is our example:

- Luke 5:16 reads, "But Jesus Himself would often slip away to the wilderness and pray."

- Luke 22:39-42, "And He came out and proceeded as was His custom to the Mount of Olives; and the disciples also followed Him. When He arrived at the place, He said to them, 'Pray that you may not enter into temptation.' And He withdrew from them about a stone's throw, and He knelt down and began to pray, saying, 'Father, if You are willing, remove this cup from Me; yet not My will, but Yours be done.'"

- Matthew 26:41, "Keep watching and praying that you may not enter into temptation; the spirit is willing, but the flesh is weak."

Page 106: "At this point in our lives, we will be close enough with God to know what we can safely share and with whom. We will be able to see others as God sees them just as Jesus saw Peter as the 'rock of the church' and not the one who denied Him."

- Give the class a moment to reflect if there is someone who has betrayed them whom they need to forgive. It is only through God's strength that we can forgive those who betray us and deny us the confidentiality we expect. We must pray to see others as God sees them.

Page 107: "We must tear off the masks and tear down the walls through our love and prayer."

Group Transparency Exercise:
Have each member of your group tell which area they struggle with the most in being transparent with others: selfishness, embarrassment, vulnerability, perfectionism, showing weaknesses/pride, trust, losing privacy, self-reliance, materialism/comparing ourselves to others. After the area is shared, have each member address how it has negatively affected them in being transparent with others.

Encourage the class to read chapter six for next week and to answer the questions at the end of the chapter.

End with prayer and/or prayer requests (if you prefer to save them until now).

End on time! ☺

WEEK 7

Chapter 6: Transparency with Love

The Plan: This lesson is intended to last one week and is the final lesson of the book.

Welcome everyone to the group. Ask for prayer requests (or this can be done at the end of the class time). Lead in prayer and ask God to bless the discussion you're about to have. Being transparent and open with a group dynamic requires the guidance and direction of the Holy Spirit. Pray specifically for this in your group. Pray for the discussion to be guided by Him. This will give some direction to the attendees that this is a sacred and special group and what is shared is not intended to go outside the room, unless permission is given.

Now that the group has come together and discussed some private issues and personal concerns, it's important to reiterate that the "safe environment" doesn't end now that the class is over. What was shared within the confines of the group continues to stay within the group. This is Christianity at its best. I remember being in a Bible study one time when a girl shared her struggle. A few years later a different group was meeting and someone else shared this same struggle. I contacted the member and asked her to contact this newer group member so they could discuss it further. Getting permission is a great sign of respect.

We have discussed being honest and transparent with ourselves (mentally & physically), with God, and with others. Now, we will dive into how we can obtain this kind of transparency and not lose our minds, or ourselves, in the process.

Page 111: "That's what this transparency thing is all about: learning to love enough to let go of ourselves."

> **Ask:** How do you see "letting go of yourself" work in your life? (e.g., putting kids/family/others before you, desiring God's plan over your own, realizing you have selfish tendencies and working to resolve those)

1. Do non-church people have a hard time seeing you as a Christian? If so, what areas of your life need to better resemble that of Christ? (e.g., TV shows/movies watched, language used, attitudes)

2. What aspect of transparency needs the most work in your life? With yourself? Expectations? God? Others? Name one way you plan to address this issue in the next week.

   - Who do you plan to hold you accountable to this issue?

Pages 112–113: Read 1 Corinthians 13.

3. According to Paul's definition of love in 1 Corinthians 13:4–8a, which area of love is easiest for you and why? Which area is the hardest?

Page 113: "Love can empower us to be transparent." Do you agree or disagree? How does this work in your life?

Recall the differences between Jim and Mary at the beginning of the book. Mary chose to share and she found freedom. Jim didn't realize his strongholds at first and chose not to share. He was miserable.

Page 116: "As we admit there are areas where we struggle, like Mary did with her group, we become transparent so others realize this seemingly perfect life still has issues."

   Ask: Do you struggle more with people who "have issues" or with those who have "seemingly perfect lives"?

Page 117: Read 1 John 4:7-12.

   4.   True love is modeled after God's love. How do you define true love and how does your definition compare to God's love in 1 John 4?

Page 118: "You see, at the core, love is not about us at all; it is about God."

   Ask: When you make love about you, and not about others, how does it fail and/or thrive?

Page 119: "This love that is shared in God's ways allows us to be more trusting of others and more transparent with them when we know their foundation of love is based upon God's love and not that of this world."

   Ask: How can you know that the other person can be trusted? (Answer: Your relationship with God must allow you to pray for that person and you must ask the Holy Spirit for a discerning heart.)

5. What is your most beloved possession? Are you ready to commit to sacrifice your most beloved possession for another's gain, as God did by sending Jesus to earth?

Ask: What would this sacrifice look like in your life and what daily steps would be required for this to happen?

6. We discussed transparency with yourself, mental expectations, physical expectations, God, and others. Are you more like Jim or Mary in each of these areas and in which area do you struggle the most?

Depending on the time you have, you could ask the class if they are more like Jim or more like Mary in each example given above.

Page 119: "When it comes down to it, though, he is ashamed to admit he knows how those like Mary feel: discontent, alone, hopeless. With a pang in his gut and a brokenness of his heart, Jim realized *he* is 'Mary' before she decided to open up her life. He, like Mary, must take the plunge and simply open up when prompted by the Holy Spirit. He will have to give himself permission to not be the strong one and allow God to be the strong one in his life."

Ask: Does this change your mind about whether you see yourself like Jim or Mary? If you are a Jim, can you relate to being a "Mary" before she opened up and was a mess?

7. Was there a turning point in your life that skewed the way you looked at love? Did this affect your relationship with God and your view of His love for you?

8. Has your view of transparency changed positively or negatively while working through this book and why?

Group Transparency Exercise:

Have each member in your group share an area of their lives that most resembles that of the world. After they give an example, have them decide which part of Paul's definition of love would help them bring this area closer to being like God and not like the world.

Page 121: Have someone read the last paragraph as you close out your discussion.

Read the quote from Christopher Wright: "Either way, faithful or unfaithful, the people of God are an open book to the world, and the world asks questions and draws conclusions." What will your book read to those around you?

End with prayer and/or prayer requests (if you prefer to save them until now). Pray that God will allow your group to continue to challenge themselves to be more open and transparent with themselves, God, and others.

End on time! ☺

Follow my blog: www.susanmsims.com for weekly writings encouraging living a transparent life!

RESOURCES

Week 1: Introduction

Personality test recommendations:

   http://www.sagestrategies.biz/documents/FiveMinutePersonalityTestf
      orclass.pdf

   http://www.16personalities.com/free-personality-test

   http://www.truity.com/test/type-finder-research-edition

See Small Group Covenant on following page.

Small Group Transparency
Covenant

1. I pledge to arrive on time and make attending all sessions of our group a priority.
2. I pledge to read and answer questions before coming to class.
3. I pledge to participate in class equally with others.
4. I pledge confidentiality to what is discussed in class and will not share without the other person's consent. I may be asked to leave should I divulge such information.
5. I pledge to respect other people in the group as we all come from different places in life and different backgrounds.
6. I pledge to be accountable to others and myself as we learn to be transparent.
7. I pledge to think about ways I can become more transparent and incorporate transparency in my life weekly, even if only with myself.

Signature: _____

Date: _____

Witness Signature: _____

Week 2: Chapter 1 – What is Transparency?

Eleanor Roosevelt quote: "No one can make you feel inferior without your consent."

Tennessee Williams quote: "We have to distrust each other. It is our only defense against betrayal."

Week 3: Chapter 2 – Mental Transparency and Expectations

Dan Miller quote: "When we are not true to ourselves, to our unique God-given characteristics, we lose the power of authenticity, creativity, imagination, and innovation. Our life becomes performance-based, setting the stage for compromise in all other areas of our lives."

Author Unknown quote: "In absence of clearly defined goals, we become strangely loyal to performing daily acts of trivia."

Proverbs 3:5 – "Trust in the LORD with all your heart and do not lean on your own understanding."

D.L. Moody quote: "There are many of us that are willing to do great things for the Lord, but few of us are willing to do little things."

Matthew 11:28 – "Come to Me, all who are weary and heavy-laden, and I will give you rest."

Week 4: Chapter 3 – Physical Health and Transparency

Lewis Thomas quote: "As a people, we have become obsessed with Health. There is something fundamentally, radically unhealthy about all of this. We do not seem to be seeking more exuberance in living as much as staving off failure, putting off dying. We have lost all confidence in the human body."

Romans 7:14-20 – "For we know that the Law is spiritual, but I am of flesh, sold into bondage to sin. For what I am doing, I do not understand; for I am not practicing what I would like to do, but I am doing the very thing I hate. But if I do the very thing I do not want to do, I agree with the Law, confessing that the Law is good. So now, no longer am I the one doing it, but sin which dwells in me. For I know that nothing good dwells in me, that is, in my flesh; for the willing is present in me, but the doing of the good is not. For the good that I want, I do not do, but I practice the very evil that I do not want. But if I am doing the very thing I do not want, I am no longer the one doing it, but sin which dwells in me."

Week 5: Chapter 4 –Transparency with God

Psalm 62:5-8 – "My soul, wait in silence for God only, for my hope is from Him. He only is my rock and my salvation, my stronghold; I shall not be shaken. On God my salvation and my glory rest; the rock of my strength, my refuge is in God. Trust in Him at all times. O people; pour out your heart before Him; God is a refuge for us."

Psalm 119:18-20, 24 – "Open my eyes, that I may behold wonderful things from Your law. I am a stranger in the earth; do not hide Your commandments from me. My soul is crushed with longing after Your ordinances at all times. Your testimonies also are my delight; they are my counselors."

Matthew 6:25,30 – "For this reason I say to you, do not be worried about your life, as to what you will eat or what you will drink; nor for your body, as to what you will put on. Is not life more than food, and the body more than clothing? But if God so clothes the grass of the field, which is alive today and tomorrow is thrown into the furnace, will He not much more clothe you? You of little faith!"

Richard Alleine quote: "The reason why we obtain no more in prayer is because we expect no more. God usually answers us according to our own hearts."

Psalm 119:26-27 – "I have told of my ways, and You have answered me; teach me Your statues. Make me understand the way of Your precepts, so I will meditate on Your wonders." These verses might be some to memorize.

Psalm 119: 33–38 – "Teach me, O LORD, the way of Your statutes, and I shall observe it to the end. Give me understanding, that I may observe Your law and keep it with all my heart. Make me walk in the path of Your commandments, for I delight in it. Incline my heart to Your testimonies and not to dishonest gain. Turn away my eyes from looking at vanity, and revive me in Your ways. Establish Your word to Your servant, as that which produces reverence for You."

Week 6: Chapter 5 –Transparency with Others

Second Corinthians 1:3-5 – "Blessed be the God and Father of our Lord Jesus Christ, the Father of mercies and God of all comfort, who comforts us in all our affliction so that we will be able to comfort those who are in any affliction with the comfort with which we ourselves are comforted by God. For just as the sufferings of Christ are ours in abundance, so also our comfort is abundant through Christ."

Matthew 7:4-5 – "Or how can you say to your brother, 'Let me take the speck out of your eye,' and behold, the log is in your own eye? You hypocrite, first take the log out of your own eye, and then you will see clearly to take the speck out of your brother's eye."

David Hume quote: "Beauty in things exists in the mind which contemplates them."

Luke 5:16 – "But Jesus Himself would often slip away to the wilderness and pray."

Luke 22:39-42 – "And He came out and proceeded as was His custom to the Mount of Olives; and the disciples also followed Him. When He arrived at the place, He said to them, 'Pray that you may not enter into temptation.' And He withdrew from them about a stone's throw, and He knelt down and began to pray, saying, 'Father, if You are willing, remove this cup from Me; yet not My will, but Yours be done.'"

Matthew 26:41 – "Keep watching and praying that you may not enter into temptation; the spirit is willing, but the flesh is weak."

Week 7: Chapter 6 –Transparency with Love

1 Corinthians 13 – "If I speak with the tongues of men and of angels, but do not have love, I have become a noisy gong or a clanging cymbal. If I have the gift of prophecy, and know all mysteries and all knowledge; and if I have all faith, so as to remove mountains, but do not have love, I am nothing. And if I give all my possessions to feed the poor, and if I surrender my body to be burned, but do not have love, it profits me nothing. Love is patient, love is kind and is not jealous; love does not brag and is not arrogant, does not act unbecomingly; it does not seek its own, is not provoked, does not take into account a wrong suffered, does not rejoice in unrighteousness, but rejoices with the truth; bears all things, believes all things, hopes all things, endures all things. Love never fails; but if there are gifts of prophecy, they will be done away; if there are tongues, they will cease; if there is knowledge, it will be done away. For we know in part and we prophesy in part; but when the perfect comes, the partial will be done away. When I was a child, I used to speak like a child, think like a child, reason like a child; when I became a man, I did away with childish things. For now we see in a mirror dimly, but then face to face; now I know in part, but then I will know fully just as I also have been fully known. But now faith, hope, love, abide these three; but the greatest of these is love.

1 John 4:7-12 – "Beloved, let us love one another, for love is from God; and everyone who loves is born of God and knows God. The one who does not love does not know God, for God is love. By this the love of God was manifested in us, that God has sent His only begotten Son into the world so that we might live through Him. In this love, not that we loved God, but that He loved us and sent His Son to be the propitiation for our sins. Beloved, if God so loved us, we also ought to love one another. No one has seen God at any time; if we love one another, God abides in us, and His love is perfected in us."

REFERENCES

Bonhoeffer, Dietrich. *Life Together.* New York: Harper & Row, Publishers, Inc., 1954.

Merriam-Webster's Dictionary of English Usage. Springfield, MA: Merriam-Webster, 1994.

Steven Kalas, "It's Easy to Ruin a Person's Reputation", *Las Vegas Review-Journal,* February 28, 2012.

"Scripture taken from the NEW AMERICAN STANDARD BIBLE®, Copyright ©1960,1962,1963,1968,1971,1972,1973,1975,1977,1995 by The Lockman Foundation. Used by permission."

ABOUT THE AUTHOR

Susan M. Sims is a stay-at-home mom of three children: Elizabeth, Erica, and David. She is happily married to her husband of eighteen years, Brian. Her desire is for all to understand the importance of being transparent as they continually grow deeper in their relationship with God and others.

Connect online with Susan in the following ways: www.susanmsims.com where you can follow her blog, Twitter @susansims97, and Facebook www.facebook.com/susansims97. She is available for speaking engagements to churches, women's groups, and retreats.